Made in United States
North Haven, CT
05 August 2022

22276323R00064